THE EPPING ONGAR RAILWAY

MALCOLM BATTEN

Acknowledgements

Thanks are due to Rodger Green for supplying material from the EOR archive and editing the text.

Thanks to Jim Connor for information taken from *Ongar 150: The Changing Face of an Essex branch Line*.

Thanks due to Andrew Cook, Martin Creese, Tony Goulding, Rodger Green, Owen Hayward, Katie Pickersgill, Richard Puttock, Geoff Silcock, and Alan Simpson for use of their photographs

Thanks also to the other photographers, known and unknown, who provided photographs from the EOR archive.

First published 2022

Amberley Publishing
The Hill, Stroud
Gloucestershire, GL5 4EP

www.amberley-books.com

Copyright © Malcolm Batten, 2022

The right of Malcolm Batten to be identified as the Author of this work has been asserted in accordance with the Copyrights, Designs and Patents Act 1988.

ISBN 978 1 3981 0784 7 (print)
ISBN 978 1 3981 0785 4 (ebook)

All rights reserved. No part of this book may be reprinted or reproduced or utilised in any form or by any electronic, mechanical or other means, now known or hereafter invented, including photocopying and recording, or in any information storage or retrieval system, without the permission in writing from the Publishers.

British Library Cataloguing in Publication Data.
A catalogue record for this book is available from the British Library.

Typesetting by SJmagic DESIGN SERVICES, India.
Printed in the UK.

Appointed GPSR EU Representative: Easy Access System Europe Oü, 16879218
Address: Mustamäe tee 50, 10621, Tallinn, Estonia
Contact Details: gpsr.requests@easproject.com, +358 40 500 3575

Contents

Introduction	4
1865–1922 The Great Eastern Period	7
1923–1947 London & North Eastern Railway	8
1948–1957 British Railways Steam Service	9
1957–1969 London Transport Electrified Service	11
1970–1994 Rundown to Closure	11
1994–2004 Pilot Developments Take Over	18
2004–07 Heritage Services Start	19
2008–12 Rebuilding Under New Ownership	23
2012 Reopening	28
2013 – 150 Years of the London Underground	33
2014	40
2015	45
2016	50
2017	54
2018	61
2019	66
2020	73
2021	76
The Bus Services	84
Features Along the Line	86
The Penny Salon	92
The Railway at Night	93
The Future	95

Introduction

The first standard-gauge heritage steam railway in Britain, the Bluebell Railway, opened in 1960. Since then, more than eighty others have opened to the public. While each of these have their individual characteristics, nearly all are former British Railways branch lines or parts of secondary routes, closed either under the 1960s Beeching axe or under subsequent cutbacks.

The 6-mile-long Epping Ongar Railway is different and unique. Despite its location in rural Essex, this was not part of the British Rail network at closure but was an electrified section of the London Underground. Its rundown and closure was a protracted affair spanning twenty-five years. On closure it was earmarked to become a heritage line, but it would be another eighteen years before it reopened in its current guise with steam and diesel traction.

The railway to Epping and Ongar was opened in 1865 by the Great Eastern Railway. The railway had earlier been built as far as Loughton in 1856 by the Eastern Counties Railway, which became part of the GER in 1862. The purpose of building was principally to bring the agricultural produce of this part of Essex to feed London's rapidly growing population. Milk became of growing importance, as there were no refrigerators, and from 1911 there was a milk train every weekday (also Saturdays from 1916) bringing some 5,000 churns of milk a week to the capital. Passenger trains initially ran to London, Fenchurch Street station or Bishopsgate as the GER's Liverpool Street terminus did not open until 1874. Originally built as single track throughout with a passing point at Epping, the section from Loughton to Epping was doubled in 1892.

In 1923 the GER passed to the London & North Eastern Railway on the grouping of railways. However, in 1935 the New Works Programme of public investment was initiated, and under this scheme the line was to be electrified to become an extension to the London Underground Central Line, which at that time ran from Ealing Broadway to Liverpool Street. Work was delayed by the Second World War, but electrification reached Epping in 1949 and the line passed to London Transport control. However, it was decided to leave the single-track section on to Ongar, always less busy, as steam worked. A passing loop and second platform were installed at North Weald. When electrification finally happened in 1957, it was done on the cheap – the line was not doubled, a proposed sub-station at Blake Hall was not built with limited traction current being provided from Epping, and the stations were not lengthened to take the eight coach trains in use south of Epping.

Therefore, the electric service ran only as a shuttle between Epping and Ongar, every twenty minutes, and therein lay the death of the line. As locals acquired cars, commuters would prefer to drive into Epping, where trains were more frequent. The line was losing money by the 1960s, and London Transport proposed closure in 1970, but this was refused – though no subsidy was offered. In 1976 Essex County Council offered to meet 25 per cent of the annual loss if a cheaper one-train service was provided. Therefore, London Transport took out the passing loop at North Weald and the signals so only one train could run, now every forty minutes. Freight services had already ended by 1966. But losses continued and again closure was proposed in 1980, and again refused, although the little-used station at Blake Hall was not so lucky and closure came in 1981. A lingering death then followed – a reduction to peak hours only, then a brief period from October 1989–April 1991 when an all-day weekday service returned. But with losses continuing to mount London Underground again proposed closure in 1993–94, suggesting a sale to a third party for the line to become a heritage railway. This time, permission was granted to close the line and the last train ran on 30 September 1994.

After closure, a proviso was made that the tracks would be retained for three years while an alternative operator was sought. The Ongar Railway Preservation Society (ORPS) was in place, and in 1995 they obtained a three-year agreement to enable them to start maintenance and clear vegetation. They proposed to run a heritage service with vintage Tube stock plus steam and diesel locomotives. However, a rival group, Pilot Developments, proposed a tri-partite scheme of a commuter service to Epping, subsidised by 'Wine and Dine' steam trains and 'Back in Time' leisure trains operated by a paying franchisee. Despite them having no experience or understanding of running a railway, London Underground announced Pilot as their preferred option and eventually sold the line in controversial circumstances to them in 1998 after a late bid was submitted.

Pilot Developments (renamed as Epping Ongar Railway in 1999) promised a commuter service within five years but were unable to achieve this as Epping station had been resignalled in 1996 so that only the new automatic Central Line 1992 stock trains could use it. The two older 1962 stock trains that they purchased to work the service remained in the platform at Ongar where they were vandalised and covered in graffiti.

With the efforts of the Epping Ongar Railway Volunteer Society (EORVS), founded in 2000, a diesel railcar service between Ongar and North Weald was operated on Sundays from October 2004. This was extended to Coopersale in 2006 after the track was lowered under the M11 bridge, which had been built in 1977 with clearance only for the Tube stock then in use. Pilot/EOR bought some steam locomotives and carriages from Finland with the intention of running their proposed 'Wine and Dine' trains, but as these were of a different track gauge (5 feet) they could not have been used without relaying all the track, and only one was ever steamed.

Pilot/EOR also put in a planning application to develop the Ongar goods yard site and possibly convert the (listed) Ongar station building to a restaurant. This application dragged on for years but part of the goods yard was eventually sold off for housing in 2007. The coal yard area was separately sold to McCarthy & Stone for retirement housing.

Under the terms of the contract selling the railway to Pilot Developments, the line had to be offered to either Essex County Council, Epping Forest District Council or London Underground if commuter services did not start within five years. The commuter service had not happened, but none of these parties were interested in taking over. After the land sell-off one of the directors submitted a bid to buy the whole railway and run the 'Wine and Dine' trains with the Finnish locos. While four other directors backed this, Roger Wright, another of the directors and former founder of Blue Triangle Buses, which he had recently sold, did not. In December 2007 the shareholders decided to settle the matter by a sealed bid process and Roger Wright's bid was successful, thus meaning he became the sole owner of the railway.

He then took the decision to close the railway for major renovation to take place. The railway was closed from 2008–12 while this took place. The track was fully relayed for main line stock with run-round loops installed and signalling fully restored. The stations were restored. This included sourcing and installing a replacement signal box at Ongar as London Transport had demolished the original one. Locomotive and stock servicing facilities were installed at North Weald and locomotives and stock acquired and restored. With works completed, the line officially reopened as a fully fledged heritage railway on 24 May 2012, the 150th anniversary of the establishment of the Great Eastern Railway in 1862.

Since then, the railway has progressed. The restoration work won the railway three heritage awards in 2012. The 150th anniversary of the start of the London Underground was celebrated in 2013 with the railway participating in the events and benefiting from the publicity. In 2014 the Underground history was again celebrated with the return of the Cravens stock Tube train that ran the last service on the line to acknowledge twenty years since closure, and ten years since first reopening. This was brought in via the still surviving connection at Epping and was propelled on the EOR by LUL Schoma diesels (because, of course, the EOR is no longer electrified). In 2015 the line was extended from Coopersale to Epping Forest – just short of Epping station, which the railway is still unable to reach due to London Underground using both platforms and the incompatibility of their signalling. Meanwhile Roger Wright's London Bus Company fleet of historic London buses provide links to the railway at North Weald and also to Shenfield for the Greater Anglia and TFL/Elizabeth Line network at Shenfield on most EOR operating days.

It is hoped that eventually the Epping Ongar Railway will once again be able to run into Epping station, if the station is rebuilt to accommodate this.

Photos are by the author except where indicated.

I remember being at the Railway in 1994 on the last night of the London Underground Central Line service with my daughter, who was aged 13 at the time. When I explained that trains had run here for almost 130 years and that this was the very last one, she became upset and I comforted her by saying, 'Don't worry, I'm sure somebody will turn this into a heritage line one day'. At the time I didn't give a thought to the possibility that it might be me!

Roger Wright – EOR owner

1865–1922 The Great Eastern Period

Ongar station building with its station house. The station was built onto the side of the platform rather than at the top of Station Road as the original intention had been for the line to continue onwards towards Dunmow. (Photographer unknown, EOR archive collection)

A contemporary commercial photo of Blake Hall station. This remote station was only built at the request of the landowners of the Blake Hall estate in return for permission to cross their land. Note the large number of milk churns on the platform, emphasising the importance of this traffic. (EOR archive collection)

1923–1947 London & North Eastern Railway

North Weald station in LNER days, one of a series of photographs printed as commercial postcards. (Photographer unknown, EOR archive collection)

Ongar station and goods yard taken in the 1930s from the top of the starter signal. There were still few houses in the area around the station at this time, although some cottages had been built in Bansons Way by the GER for railway workers in 1892 and 1912. Houses would be built in the field to the left of the engine shed in 1957 (now Bowes Drive). (Photographer unknown, EOR archive collection)

1948–1957 British Railways Steam Service

After electrification reached Epping in 1949, the service onwards to Ongar remained steam worked until 1957. Ongar trains departed from platform 1. (Photographer unknown, EOR archive collection)

Services were worked by push-pull-fitted ex-GER F5 2-4-2Ts, so there was no need to run round at the end of each journey. The locomotives were always at the Epping end. Here No. 67218 awaits departure from Ongar. (T. Wright, EOR archive collection)

F5 No. 67200 departs North Weald for Epping on 23 March 1957. This was the only passing point on the line and the busiest station as it served the North Weald RAF airfield. In the background are masts of the 1920 Marconi's Wireless Telegraph Company radio transmitting station. (Photographer unknown, EOR archive collection)

A postcard produced by the EOR showing Blake Hall on the last day of steam passenger services, 16 November 1957. (EOR)

1957–1969 London Transport Electrified Service

A three-car train of Standard stock leaving Ongar for Epping. The entrance to the goods yard, then still in use, is to the right. (Photographer unknown, EOR archive collection)

1970–1994 Rundown to Closure

1962 Tube stock replaced the pre-war Standard stock at the end of 1966. Here a four-car set stands at Ongar c. 1971. The run-round loop, no longer needed since the withdrawal of freight services in 1966 has been lifted. (Reg Batten)

The Ongar signal box had closed on 23 March 1969 but was still in situ at this stage. It would subsequently be demolished. (Reg Batten)

The redundant goods shed seen on the same occasion. The goods yard had closed in April 1966. (Reg Batten)

Blake Hall station was closed on 31 October 1981. It was the least used station on the Underground with only about six regular commuters and had been closed on Sundays since 1966. When this view was taken in 1985, the building was boarded up but the lamp posts were still in place, as was the frame where the LT roundel nameboard had been in place. The station was granted Grade II listed status in April 1984. (Alan Simpson)

After closure, unofficially, train drivers had still been picking up and dropping off the few 'regulars' from Blake Hall. London Transport management eventually found out about this and sent out workmen to demolish the platform and fence off the station building! This view from 1987 shows the result as a train for Ongar approaches. (Alan Simpson)

On 30 October 1989 an all-week timetable was restored, and Ongar station is suitably decorated to promote this. However, demand did not materialise and peak-hours-only operation returned from April 1991. (Alan Simpson)

Despite the rundown, the 125th anniversary of the opening of the line was celebrated in 1990. A spotless train of Cravens stock in red livery was used and a good turnout by locals and enthusiasts is evident in this view at North Weald. The passing loop had been redundant since the introduction of a one-train service in 1976 and was lifted in July 1978. (Alan Simpson)

The Cravens stock crosses the Cripsey Brook viaduct approaching Ongar. The 1960 Cravens stock originally comprised three eight-car trains, each of two four-car units. The driving motor cars were new and in unpainted aluminium, while the trailers were pre-1938 stock modified and painted silver to match. They were used to trial automatic train operation on the Woodford–Hainault shuttle. By 1990 only three three-car sets remained (now with 1938 stock trailers) and two of these were repainted red for the Epping–Ongar shuttle in 1990–01. (Alan Simpson)

As closure seemed imminent the Ongar Railway Preservation Society had been formed with the aim of taking over the line. They had gained access to do some preliminary work, including restoring the closed signal box at North Weald. This view from 1992 also shows the concrete footbridge that would later be replaced. (Alan Simpson)

Left: On 17 May 1993 an evening peak train from Ongar arrives at Epping formed of a four-car 1962 Tube stock set. In the 1990s London Underground claimed that only around a hundred passengers a day were being carried. There was an annual loss of £184,000 and a subsidy of £7 per passenger.

Below: Shortly afterwards, the train departs for Ongar as an eight-car train waits in the other platform for London and beyond.

It is 30 September 1994 and the last day of trains from Epping to Ongar, worked by Cravens 1960 stock car Nos 3909 and 3907 with 1938 stock trailer car No. 4927. In the other platform at Epping is one of the new 1992 stock trains introduced to the Central Line in 1993. On 13 July 1993 one of these eight-car trains made a test run between Epping and Ongar although eight-car trains were never used in passenger service. (Alan Simpson)

Ongar station after closure. As can be seen there was just the single track, the signal box was long gone and the station signs had been removed. (Photographer unknown, EOR archive collection)

The platform side of Ongar station after closure. The station building and coal offices had been listed Grade II in July 1984. (Photographer unknown, EOR archive collection)

1994–2004 Pilot Developments Take Over

In 1996 Pilot Developments stated publicly that they wished to work with ORPS to produce a joint bid for the line and offered for ORPS to run 'Back in Time' experiences, but ORPS rejected this as any arrangement would be on Pilot's terms and ORPS would be expected to pay an annual fee of £250,000 for the 'franchise'. After the sale to Pilot, ORPS continued to publicly criticise their plans and as a result Pilot denied them access to the railway sites. Eventually members drifted away and the society was disbanded.

The Journal of **Ongar Railway Preservation Society** Issue No. 13 ~ Autumn, 1996

The autumn 1996 cover of *Keeping Tracks*, the journal of the ORPS, showing a notice board placed at the entrance road to Ongar station prohibiting entry. (EOR archive collection)

Two 1962 stock Tube trains were obtained by Pilot Developments and moved from Ruislip depot to Ongar in October 1996. But they were not allowed to run into Epping and a proposed platform to be called Epping Glade, some 370 yards north of Epping, never materialised. The Tube trains remained at Ongar, where they were vandalised and covered in graffiti. (Tim Stedman in *Keeping Tracks*, EOR archive collection)

2004–07 Heritage Services Start

> I paid my £4, was handed my ticket and walked onto the platform. There was no gift shop, neither was there a coffee shop to serve waiting passengers.
>
> But for those at Ongar station for the 11 a.m. train, such matters were probably not even in their thoughts.
>
> For them it was the fact that ten years and ten days after London Underground closed the branch line, they were witnessing its revival.
>
> (*Epping Forest Guardian*, October 2004)

The Epping Ongar Railway Volunteer Society (EORVS) was formed in 2000 and aided Pilot Developments/EOR in repairing the track and buildings. They then acquired Class 117 DMU driving motor cars 51384 and 51342, which originally formed part of a three-car set on Paddington suburban services. This entered service on 10 October 2004 in EOR blue and white livery, running five return trips between Ongar and North Weald on most Sundays. Here it approaches North Weald on 2 October 2005. The electric conductor rails had been removed by now.

The DMU stands at North Weald on the same day. There is only a single track, as the passing loop was lifted in 1978. The signal box is boarded up and the concrete footbridge installed by London Transport *c.* 1949 remains in place. A Sunday vintage bus service linking Ongar station with Epping station was instigated by a board member Mick Bidell, who owned Imperial Buses of Rainham, and this took the redundant route number 339 that once served the same roads.

At Ongar, the DMU stands beside the Finnish locomotives. There were four of these initially – all of different designs. A length of 5-foot-gauge track was laid alongside the platform road at Ongar where these and the carriages were located. This is a Pacific 4-6-2.

Finnish 0-6-0T No.794 leads 2-8-0 No. 1134. The Pacific is behind these two. The Finnish locomotives were owned and brought in by Nigel Sill, one of the directors of the Epping Ongar Railway.

The fourth Finnish locomotive was 2-8-2 No. 1060. They arrived from 1999 onwards.

Although there were four Finnish locomotives, only two carriages were delivered to Ongar. If these locomotives and carriages were to have run it would have meant relaying all the track to 5-foot gauge (or even dual gauge if the DMU was to be retained, and if such a combination of gauges was even feasible). Even then there would also have been expensive modifications needed at bridges and platforms to meet clearance problems associated with the larger loading gauge of the Finnish stock.

Only one of the Finnish locomotives was steamed – TK3 type 2-8-0 No. 1151, which was brought in later in December 2005 and operated over a short length of 5-foot-gauge track in the yard at Ongar in April 2007. (Michael Hardy, EOR archive collection)

Acquired in 2005 was this Drewry 0-4-0 diesel shunter for maintenance trains. It was named *Heather* and numbered D1995 after the owner's daughter and her date of birth.

2008–12 Rebuilding Under New Ownership

The Finnish locomotives and carriages would not form part of the new plans so these were initially removed. For a while some were moved to the remaining section of Ongar goods yard, where the 2-8-2 No. 1060 is seen with one of the carriages on 6 July 2008. This has since been sold on and is now located on a farm at Weeting in Norfolk. Also note the ex-London Transport bus RTL672 awaiting restoration.

The 4-6-2 Pacific is seen with the other carriage, both in a rather dilapidated condition. This is the only one of the Finnish locomotives that has remained at the railway (see p. 88).

All of the track was relaid and set at the right height for main line stock rather than Tube stock at the stations. Here, a point for the sidings at the north end of North Weald station is being installed on 7 February 2010. Some track sections came from near Custom House station on the North Woolwich branch, closed in December 2006. At Ongar, a double slip at the entrance to the goods yard area was purchased to mirror what was originally there. (Richard Puttock)

On the same day, the trackbed at North Weald has been prepared for tracklaying. The signal box had been repainted but more work needed to be done and shutters were fitted over the windows in case of vandalism. (Richard Puttock)

The LT-era concrete footbridge at North Weald was badly decayed and needed replacing. The EOR were presented with a GER lattice iron bridge, which had been rescued from near South Woodford (Churchfields) in 1999 by the chairman of the Ongar Railway Preservation Society. The span section of this awaits erection alongside sections of track, again in February 2010. The stairs were damaged when the bridge was dismantled and needed to be rebuilt when the bridge was re-erected by EORVS volunteers. (Richard Puttock)

The station buildings were restored to period colours – at Ongar to Great Eastern brown and stone, at North Weald to LNER green and cream. Period-style notice boards have also been fitted. (Richard Puttock)

As the original signal box at Ongar had been demolished by London Transport, a replacement of the same design was needed. Luckily a suitable example was found at Spellbrook near Bishop's Stortford. This was dismantled and the top was taken for storage at the Mangapps Railway Museum, Burnham-on-Crouch, until ready to be reconstructed at Ongar. The lever frame however is the Ongar original, as this had been saved and kept in a barn.

A public pre-opening day was held at North Weald on 3 July 2011, the day of the bus rally at North Weald Airfield, from which a bus link was provided. This was a big success with a total of 1,168 visitors being recorded. Class 37 diesel D6729 and Class 03 No. 03170 stand in the platforms at North Weald. Note that the platforms are not yet fully surfaced.

D6729 ran shuttles south to Coopersale with a single coach and brake van. The Class 03 ran up to Marconi Bridge in the Ongar direction.

At the southern end of the station the trackwork into the bay platform is yet to be completed.

2012 Reopening

On 24 May 2012 the culmination of four years of hard work came together when the Epping Ongar Railway formally reopened as a steam and diesel heritage line. At the opening, owner Roger Wright stated, 'The extensive works on the restoration of the track, signals, stations and rolling stock undertaken by volunteers aged from 18 to 82 has been key to the return of steam to the railway.'

The EOR's flagship locomotive, GWR Hall class No. 4953 *Pitchford Hall*, breaks through the banner at North Weald to mark the official launch of services. Public services began the following day. (Rodger Green)

As the EOR's other main line steam locomotive, GWR 41XX 2-6-2T No. 4141, was still undergoing overhaul at the Llangollen Railway, they loaned the EOR another GWR loco, 0-6-0PT 6430, to work the services. Here she waits to depart from North Weald on the first weekend of services, 26 May 2012.

Seen from the signal box, No. 6430 arrives at Ongar on 26 May.

No. 6430 shared steam workings with *Pitchford Hall*, seen here at North Weald on 1 July.

The first steam locomotive to be acquired by the EOR in 2012 was 1919 Hawthorn Leslie & Co. 0-6-0ST No. 3437 *Isabel*. This was new to ICI Foodstuff's Blackley Dye Plant, where she worked until 1969. Seen at Ongar on 1 July.

Arriving in May 2012 was Barclay 0-4-0ST *Victory*. This former Royal Navy Chatham Dockyard shunter had been restored at the Colne Valley Railway. She is seen at Ongar on 24 June but has since departed from the railway. (Richard Puttock)

Unlike the steam fleet, some of the diesels have East Anglian connections. Class 37 D6729 entered service at Stratford on 3 October 1961, working trains between Liverpool Street and Norwich or Harwich Parkston Quay. Withdrawal from the national network came in 2007.

Not looking so smart at this stage was the railway's Class 31 No. 31438, which has charge of the ex-Southern Region 3-CIG EMU unit 1498 (since sold on) at North Weald on 26 August. Built in 1959 as D5557, the Class 31 was initially allocated to Ipswich. A repaint in BR blue took place during 2013.

One of the two Class 03 diesel shunters owned, No. 03170 acts as yard pilot on 26 May. Built as D2170 at Swindon Works, this entered service at Hull Dairycoates depot in 1960. As No. 03170 it was the last Class 03 to be converted and overhauled at Swindon works before it closed. When withdrawn in 1989 this was one of the last three examples of the class in service. Arrival at the EOR came in 2010.

2013 – 150 Years of the London Underground

2013 was significant as it marked 150 years since the opening of the first part of the London Underground – the world's first underground railway. The section from Paddington to Farringdon, which now forms part of the Circle and Hammersmith & City lines, opened with steam operation in 1863 and was built by 'cut and cover' to main line dimensions. The anniversary was celebrated with a variety of celebrations not only on the Underground but also on other heritage railways that helped with preparing for the events by supplying or restoring stock and locomotives used. The EOR, as a former part of the Underground, was also a full party to the celebrations.

Visiting for the event was former Metropolitan Railway E class 0-4-4T No. 1 built in 1898. Normally preserved at the Buckinghamshire Railway Centre, this had performed on the Underground at 'Steam on the Met' events from 1989, and indeed also earlier in 2013. Here she enters North Weald on 30 June.

MET No. 1 is seen again at Marconi Bridge on the approach to North Weald on June 30. The bridge is so named because from 1920 to *c.* 1990 there was a radio transmitting station with a series of masts nearby.

A number of vintage carriages were loaned to the railway for the event. Metropolitan Railway four-wheel coach No. 353 was restored for the London Transport Museum and used on both their own celebrations on the Underground and also on other participating heritage lines.

Also visiting was former GWR 4575 class 2-6-2T No. 5521. In May 2013 this had been repainted in London Transport livery and numbered L150 for the anniversary celebrations. This is fitted with a Westinghouse pump to work with both vacuum and air-braked stock. Here she approaches Marconi Bridge from the North Weald direction. (Geoff Silcock)

The EOR's own GWR 2-6-2T No. 4141 had not been ready until December 2012. Now in regular service, she was renumbered as 6141 for the celebrations. The 61XX class were generally similar but worked on Paddington suburban services.

Also visiting the EOR in 2013 was the sole surviving Gresley N2 0-6-2T, which is owned by the Gresley Society. These locomotives were used on suburban services from Kings Cross or Moorgate.

The Underground 150 Years headboard carried by some of the locomotives during the events. (Richard Puttock)

Another of the EOR's diesel fleet, BR Class 25 D7523 at North Weald on 7 July 2013. This joined the railway in 2011 and worked in 2012–13, but with the bodywork suffering from rust, it was sent away to the Battlefield Line in 2014 for restoration work and has not returned since. Also bowing out in August 2013 was *Pitchford Hall* as she was due a full overhaul and new boiler certificate.

Ex-Southern Region 3-CIG EMU unit No. 1498 was in use at this time as coaching stock and is propelled into North Weald. The crossing gates were acquired from Chitt's Hill on the London side of Colchester. This was the last manually worked crossing on the Norwich main line and the gates became redundant as part of a resignalling scheme.

A first Diesel Gala was held in September 2013, at which resident Thumper DEMU No. 205205 made its debut. Originally built as No. 1111 in 1957 this was bought from the North Yorkshire Moors Railway in 2009. This was the only unit to have been modernised with a corridor connection. Network SouthEast livery is carried.

The Southern Region theme was further enhanced by a visit from 'Slim Jim' Class 33 No. 33202 *Dennis G. Robinson*.

Class 47 No. 47635 *Jimmy Milne* arrived as a guest locomotive for the September 2013 Gala but was acquired and has remained on the EOR ever since. Jimmy Milne was a former General Secretary of the Scottish Trades Union Congress. No. 47635 has since been refurbished and repainted in large logo blue livery.

The two resident Class 03s are seen at Ongar, along with D6729 about to run round its train. No. 03119 has a cut-down cab for working over the restricted Burry Port & Gwendraeth Valley branch.

2014

2014 marked twenty years since closure of the line, and this was suitably celebrated in September when the last Underground train to work on the line, which had itself been preserved, returned to the railway and once again worked through to Ongar – albeit this time propelled by diesel.

A visitor for the Diesel Gala in April was Class 20 No. 20048. Here this waits to depart from North Weald for Ongar. Note that the footbridge is still incomplete at this stage with the steps not yet in place.

The June Steam Gala saw three visiting locomotives performing as well as resident Prairie tank No. 4141. LMS 3F 0-6-0T No. 47406 arrives at North Weald, where the signalman is waiting to take the single line token. This was a visitor from the Great Central Railway.

Visiting LMS Black 5 No. 45379 from the Mid-Hants Railway passes under Marconi Bridge on the approach to North Weald.

The blue and grey stock is taken back to Ongar by resident GWR 41XX 2-62T No. 4141, again at Marconi Bridge.

The other visiting locomotive was former London & South Western Railway Beattie 0-4-0WT No. 30585, seen in the yard at North Weald. Three of this diminutive class from 1863 survived into BR ownership and were used on the Wenford Bridge branch in Cornwall until 1962. Two of the three survived into preservation. (Richard Puttock)

Among the other special events during the year was a 1940s weekend. This impressive display of memorabilia was among the exhibits. (Richard Puttock)

Right: The return of the Cravens stock Tube cars. The train that had worked the last service train in September 1994 had been preserved by Cravens Heritage Trains. The Tube cars and diesels were brought in over the surviving connection to the Central Line at Epping during the night – the only occasion since reopening that this connection has been used. (Owen Hayward)

Below: The Cravens stock stands in the platform at North Weald with the 'Silent Whistle' headboard as carried in the cab window on the last day.

As the EOR is of course no longer electrified, the Tube train was not taking power but was hauled or propelled by a pair of London Underground's Tube profile Schoma diesels. No. 3 *Claire* leads as the stock enters North Weald. The other pair of the Schoma diesels were on display at Ongar.

Sharing the duties appropriately was Metropolitan No. 1 making a repeat visit. This also made some demonstration runs of an engineering works train through the North Weald station area.

On September 26, a rededication was made of the '0.0 km' plate sign at Ongar. This sign, mounted above the buffer stop was (and still is) the starting point for all distance measurements on the Underground network. Railway owner Roger Wright is on the right. (Richard Puttock)

2015

More celebrations in 2015 – this time 150 years since the opening of the branch to Ongar by the Great Eastern Railway in 1865. In time for the April celebrations, the running line was extended from Coopersale to Epping Forest, just short of Epping station.

A Steam Gala in April saw a visit from Class J72 No. 69023, normally based on the North Yorkshire Moors Railway. This is painted in North Eastern Railway green. Despite the design dating from 1898 a further batch, Nos 69001–28, were built by BR between 1949 and 1951. It was being prepared for service at North Weald.

Also of North Eastern Railway design is diminutive Y7 class 0-4-0T No. 985. Here she works an equally diminutive train of one hopper wagon and 'Shark' brake van approaching Marconi Bridge.

Representing the home fleet, GWR 41XX 2-6-2T No. 4141 stands at North Weald. The Y7 and its train are in the bay platform. 4141 would later be withdrawn from traffic for overhaul in 2015 with firebox problems.

Another visitor at the April Diesel Gala was Great Western Railway's Old Oak Common-based Class 08 No. 08483, seen working with the Thumper DEMU as carriages. (Owen Hayward)

A second Steam Gala in June had a GWR flavour with the visit of three ex-GWR locomotives alongside resident 4141. The crew of Manor class 4-6-0 No. 7820 *Dinmore Manor* prepare to take the single line token from the signalman on departure from Ongar. Pity about the out-of-character road cone – apparently to warn of a loose coping stone on the platform. (Richard Puttock)

Making a repeat visit, Pannier tank No. 6430 awaits departure from North Weald as No. 4141 drifts in with a train from Ongar.

Also visiting was auto-fitted 14XX 0-4-2T No. 1450, which came with a Great Western autocoach. This enabled it to run in push-pull mode to Epping Forest where normally, as there is no run-round facility, another locomotive needs to be added to the rear of a train to pull it back to North Weald. The train is seen in the forest section. (Geoff Silcock)

Seen from Watkins Bridge, the tail lamp on the coach shows that this train is heading back to North Weald. (Geoff Silcock)

A view back through the driving windows of the autocoach. (Richard Puttock)

Pannier tank No. 6430 was also equipped for working with the autocoach. This view shows the very different character of this end of the line, which runs into Epping Forest, compared with North Weald to Ongar, which runs mainly through fields. (Geoff Silcock)

2016

The April 2016 Diesel Gala brought another visiting Class 20 – this time D8059. This is at North Weald along with the Thumper on 23 April.

Also visiting was this Class 08 shunter in early BR black livery, numbered as 13236, from Nemesis Rail, Burton. Here it brings a train from Epping Forest back into North Weald. D8059 is on the rear of the train.

Resident Ruston 0-4-0 diesel shunter in early BR black livery as No. 2957. BR had a pair of similar locomotives, D2957–8, built in 1956 at Stratford until *c.* 1967. This was in the headshunt at Ongar on 10 June. The locomotive had been bought in the early 2000s for track maintenance trains. Now being of limited use, this was sold in 2016. The disused Plasser & Theurer tamping machine just visible was also sold.

The June Steam Gala brought superpower in the form of 9F 2-10-0 No. 92214 from the Great Central Railway. Here it makes a spirited departure from Ongar. (Geoff Silcock)

As the 9F was painted green (a feature only carried in BR days by No. 92220 *Evening Star*) it was decided to name it *Ongar Star* for the duration. However, the owners did not permit this, so instead the nameplates that had been made were fitted to another visiting engine, Hudswell Clarke 0-6-0T *Jennifer* from the Llangollen Railway, taken at Ongar.

Another visitor was BR 2-6-4T No. 80072 from the Llangollen Railway. This has got the signal to depart from North Weald. The DMU car No. 51384, recently painted but as yet unlined and not numbered, has been employed as an additional carriage.

The Gresley Society's N2 0-6-2T, liveried as GNR No. 1744, was also back at the EOR and arrives at North Weald during the Steam Gala. The GWR saloon coach at the head of the train left the railway in 2017.

After steam superpower with the 9F, it was the turn for diesel superpower at the September Gala with the visit of Deltic No. 55019 *Royal Highland Fusilier*. The footbridge at North Weald had now been completed, offering a new vantage point for photography. In the sidings is Peak No. 45132, a long-term restoration project for its owning group who brought it to the EOR from the Mid Hants Railway in September 2014.

Also visiting was another Class 20, this time No. 20142 painted in London Transport livery, having been used in the Underground's celebration services. Alongside is another visitor, Railway Support Services (RSS) Class 08 shunter No. 08683.

2017

The April 2017 Diesel Gala saw yet another Class 20 visiting the railway. This time No. 8001 owned by the Class 20 Locomotive Society. When new in 1957 the first of this class were allocated to Devon's Road, Bow, in East London, which was BR's first locoshed to be 'dieselised'.

Above: Also visiting was Class 33 D6501 in original livery without the later yellow warning panel. This is arriving at North Weald, passing under the footbridge completed the previous year.

Right: A Victorian weekend was held in June. A pair of actors in Victorian costume engage in conversation outside the gents at the 1865-built Ongar station as 1898-built MET No. 1 runs round.

The same weekend saw a brief visit by newly restored BR 2-6-4T No. 80078 after appearing at the Mangapps Railway earlier in the month. Not exactly Victorian but an attractive visitor. Here it passes the former Blake Hall station.

August featured a weekend with visiting traction engines and steam cars at North Weald. Burrell showman's road locomotive No. 4999 stands outside the station. New to Henry Thurston Jr in 1922 and named *Margaret*, this spent twenty years preserved in Holland where it was named *Stokomolief* before being repatriated. (Richard Puttock)

The September Diesel Gala saw a visit from Class 26 D5343. The BR blue livery was well matched with the rake of coaches in BR blue/grey, as seen on arrival at Ongar.

Also visiting was Class 50 No. 50026 *Indomitable* in Network SouthEast livery. Seen arriving at North Weald, restoration work is continuing on the Peak alongside.

At the Steam Gala a week later, resident *Isabel* appeared newly overhauled and outshopped in black livery. This was done as there was not enough time to fully line out the locomotive in time for the gala.

There was a repeat visit by 3F tank No. 47406, last seen in 2014. This is departing from Ongar on 30 September.

The Mid-Hants Railway's Ivatt 2MT 2-6-2T was due to work throughout the three-day gala but only arrived in time for the Sunday, 1 October. Here it waits departure time from Ongar. The GWR 'Fruit D' van is marshalled at the front of the train.

The Ivatt stayed on for the following weekend, during which it ran in the guise of No. 41268. This was in tribute to loco engineer Tony Goulding's late father who had passed out as a fireman on this loco when based at Leicester Midland (15C) depot.

Snow is not often a feature in Essex, but a snowstorm during the 'Santa Specials' on 10 December led to this seasonal scene as the N2 0-6-2T arrives at North Weald from Epping Forest. (Geoff Silcock)

This frosty afternoon scene was captured at Ongar with the N2 on 28 December during the post-Christmas 'Mince Pie Specials'. (Geoff Silcock)

2018

An interesting arrival for the Steam Gala was the American-built S160 2-8-0 No. 5197 from the Churnet Valley Railway. Like all other visitors to the railway this was brought in on a low-loader, which is seen negotiating the entrance to Station Road in North Weald. (Tony Goulding)

The S160 faced north towards Ongar and is seen laying over in the loop before taking the next train back to North Weald and Epping Forest.

Left: Visiting from the Severn Valley Railway was GWR 0-6-0ST No. 813, originally Port Talbot Railway No. 26. A water tower and crane had now been installed at Ongar in 2017 and the crew are taking advantage of this.

Below: Another arrival in 2018 for the season was Hunslet Austerity 0-6-0ST No. 3883 *Lord Phil*, also seen at Ongar.

Right: During the Vintage Steam Rally, some of the traction engines went on a road run and this gave an opportunity for this posed shot at Coopersale Bridge with Metropolitan No. 1 and Fowler Road locomotive *AD 9200 Sir Douglas*. Only the warning sign on the bridge with metric measurements detracts from the vintage image. (Owen Hayward)

Below: During 2018, London Underground Ltd donated a 1959 stock driving motor car – No. 1031, as used on the Northern Line until 2000. This had been retained at Morden depot until disposed of due to an upgrade project. The Tube car was positioned at North Weald with the intention of it being used for a museum display. However, as a result of asbestos content, no work has been possible on this to date.

The Bus Rally on 9 September had a theme of the 'London Bus Reshaping Plan' of 1968, which saw a start of replacing double-deck buses with one-man-operated AEC Merlin and later Swift single-deckers. These proved to be unreliable and most were sold off after a relatively short life. Some of the surviving buses line up in the field at North Weald.

Visiting for the September Diesel Gala was the only survivor of the somewhat short-lived and unsuccessful Class 17 Clayton Type 1. D8568's home is the Chinnor & Princes Risborough Railway. It was built in 1964 and withdrawn from BR service in 1971. Here it runs round at Ongar.

In October 2018 the Railcar Association held their twenty-third convention at the EOR. This led to a visit by Class 121 'Bubblecar' single car DMU 55033. This awaits departure from a deserted Ongar platform – a photo that could have almost been taken on a pre-Beeching BR branch line in the early 1960s.

A return visit by BR 2-6-4T No. 80078 saw it employed on the 'Santa Specials'. The whole train has been drawn up for the loco to use the water column. This is because No. 80078 will not be running round – the train is top and tailed with a diesel, which will haul it on the return journey.

2019

The 2019 season got off with the February Bus Rally, which had the theme 'Green Line'. Visiting vehicles included 1938-built T499 preserved by Ensignbus, and 1939-built TF77 from the London Transport Museum. These were displayed at North Weald and, as can be seen, the weather was excellent.

Locomotives are often in use on non-public days for maintenance work, and here No. 8001 stands at Ongar while the track maintenance gang take a break. This Class 20 is now on long-term stay at the EOR.

The rain has stopped, the sun has come out again and the crew of visiting Class 25 D7612 await departure from Ongar on 4 May. To the left the covers protect a pair of Gresley LNER teak coaches awaiting restoration.

For the June Steam Gala, the Scottish Railway Preservation Society's Caledonian 0-4-4T had been booked to attend, and leaflets had been printed to this effect. An interesting pairing of this in Caledonian blue and resident 0-4-4T MET No. 1 in maroon was in the offing. However, the Scottish loco had failed while at the previous stop on its itinerary, the Gloucestershire Warwickshire Railway, and they sent GWR 42XX 2-8-0T No. 4270 as a substitute, seen here arriving at Ongar. No. 4270 became the eighth locomotive designed by the GWR or one of its predecessor companies to run on the EOR since 2012.

The American S160 returned, this time for a longer stay including the 1940s weekend. This time it was facing south and is seen here at North Weald during that event. (Richard Puttock)

Isabel had now been painted in lined red again in 2018 and was giving brake van rides with the 'Shark' at North Weald during the 1940s weekend.

The Class 45 Peak No. 45132 had been promised for various Diesel Galas but the owners had not succeeded in getting it into running order. In March 2019 the engine was successfully started up and the loco moved to the running shed area. Unfortunately on a test run in August there was a smell of burning and it was realised that the generator would have to be stripped out for attention, so it was returned to the sidings at North Weald.

Over the August bank holiday weekend Metropolitan No. 1 left the EOR temporarily to return to its home base of the Buckinghamshire Railway Centre, who were holding an anniversary event. To cover its absence, they sent this former NCB 0-6-0ST. The silver-coloured shed building was installed in the early 2000s on the site of the original brick locomotive shed and contains the original pit. A long-term aim is to build a replacement brick shed.

A major bus rally held on 8 September coincided with an open day at the premises of Lodge's Coaches, who were celebrating ninety-nine years of business. Three Bedford OBs from Lodge's heritage fleet conveyed visitors from the EOR to their premises. The three Bedfords pose at North Weald before departure along with the London Bus Company's RF136, which was specially repainted in this one-off livery. This had been applied to a modified RF by London Transport as a back-up to the RC class in these colours on Green Line route 705, but was not approved and never ran as such in public.

The main themes of the Bus Rally were marking eighty years since RT1 first entered service and forty years since the RTs and RFs ended service. At the end of the afternoon there was a road run and run past along the approach road to North Weald airfield. The London Bus Company's RT3871 enters the roundabout near the airfield entrance. Finally, the buses ran to Harlow Garden Centre for one last line-up.

The September Diesel Gala brought a visit from a Warship loco – D821 *Greyhound*. The driver looks back for the flag to depart at Ongar.

The end of September was a significant anniversary as it was twenty-five years since the railway was closed by London Transport on 30 September 1994. This was suitably celebrated with an exhibition at the Penny Salon gallery. On 27 September, the nearest operating day to the anniversary, MET No. 1 ran bearing the 'Last Train' headboard carried by the Tube train twenty-five years earlier.

Another significant event at the end of a momentous year was the return of *Pitchford Hall* after overhaul at the GCR. Now painted in BR lined black and facing north, it was employed on 'Santa Special' duties and arrives at Ongar on 15 December in crisp winter sunshine.

A photo charter was organised for 30 December with the newly repainted *Pitchford Hall*, with a daytime run and night shoot. The weather was excellent, as can be seen in this scene taken between Blake Hall and Ongar. (Martin Creese)

2020

2020 was the *annus horibilis* most people will want to forget. While events initially ran as normal, rumours of a new pandemic soon became a reality and the country was plunged into lockdown measures from late March. Easter, normally one of the busiest times of the year, was lost. Later relaxations saw services resume from 1 August, and there was some optimism that Christmas services would run. Preparations were made to run light trains, as these had proved successful on other railways the previous year. But rising Covid cases led to a new major nationwide lockdown after the first weekend of December and the railway had to close once again.

The only main gala event before lockdown was the bus rally on 23 February. The theme was fifty years since London Transport's Country Area and Green Line coaches became part of the new National Bus Company, named London Country Bus Services. A highlight was the visit of preserved Southdown Leyland PD3 BUF 272C, sporting London Country NBC fleet names. Three of these vehicles were bought by London Country in 1975 because of vehicle shortages and worked from Godstone garage in Southdown livery. Here the bus is turning into Station Road, North Weald, after working a former local area route.

Completed in March just before lockdown was the repaint of Class 03 No. 03170 from blue to original green livery as D2170. The shunter was built at Swindon Works and research showed that it was originally numbered in a style unique to Swindon, with a dot between the D and the number, which was faithfully recreated by Geoff Silcock when he applied the transfers.

On 29 September, *Isabel* got a rare outing, working shuttles through North Weald with a single coach and Shark brake van.

The following weekend, *Isabel* should have run again but was failed, so D2170 took over the duties. This is seen on 5 September.

On the same day, the DMU, mainstay of services since resumption, departs North Weald for Ongar. This is the original DMU that was first painted blue (see p. 19), but driving motor car 51384 is currently paired with Class 121 driving trailer car 56287. This is on long-term loan from the Colne Valley Railway as car 51342 needs major restoration work.

Pitchford Hall was steamed on 28–30 October. On 30 October she makes a rare non-stop pass through North Weald towards Epping Forest. The Class 31 is on the tail to bring the train back. Note that the *Hall* now faced south. When she first returned in 2019 she faced north, but after a trip away to the Great Central Railway's Steam Gala in February 2020 she was unloaded facing south.

2021

2021 started with the country still in lockdown and the railway unable to operate, and again Easter was lost. In February 2021 two further steam locomotives arrived at the railway as long-term restoration projects. These are a pair of Robert Stephenson & Hawthorn 0-6-0STs, works numbers 7667 and 7761 of 1950 and 1954. Originally these both worked for Stewart & Lloyds steelworks at Corby. As the restrictions were gradually eased, public reopening was able to start from 22 May with the DMU. A late decision to run with steam over the spring bank holiday proved to be a roaring success with a combination of steam traction and sunny weather bringing in the visitors. After that the railway continued to thrive, particularly with the programme of children's events, and once the remaining restrictions were lifted. The enthusiast gala events were then concentrated in September–October after the school holidays. The year would be completed with the light trains and 'Santa Specials', for which online bookings had been especially strong.

In the run-up to reopening there was a programme of 'sprucing-up' the stations and some test runs for the crews and station staff. On 15 May GWR 56XX 0-6-2T No. 5619 was steamed for these runs and stands in North Weald station. This had arrived on loan for the Christmas season in November 2020, but due to the lockdown had hardly seen any use.

The Llangollen Railway had got into financial difficulties and had to sell off part of its stock. The EOR took advantage of this to purchase an additional coach, BR MK1 TSO No. 4947, allowing full separate rakes of blue/grey and maroon/'blood and custard' to be operated. The coach is seen on arrival at North Weald on 23 May awaiting unloading. The low-loader was also used to turn *Pitchford Hall* to once again face north.

The spring bank holiday weekend 29–31 May was used as a first attempt to bring back steam operation. No. 5619 was the locomotive in steam and is seen on a departure from North Weald. The DMU waits in the other platform to form a service to Epping Forest. (Geoff Silcock)

Above left: *Pitchford Hall* got her first outing of the year on 26 June. Here she backs down over the level crossing onto her train at North Weald under the watchful eye of a porter.

Above right: An early 1960s view on some BR branch line? No, North Weald with the DMU and Class 03 in the bay platform. Being printed in black and white gives that period flavour. The DMU remains the mainstay of most non-event days, providing the services to Epping Forest while the steam or diesel loco runs between Ongar and North Weald. (Richard Puttock)

Left: The first of the season's children's events got under way on 11 July with a visit from Peppa Pig and George. This was hugely popular and later repeated. It was a rare public outing for D2170, which was tasked with hauling Peppa and George on an open wagon through North Weald station, stopping at regular intervals so that the families lined up along the platform could take photos of their children with the characters.

The first EOR Bus Rally since February 2019 took place on 5 September. The theme was 'seventy years of the RF' and a selection of the visiting members of the type can be seen lined up in the field at North Weald.

One of the few vehicles in the London Bus Company fleet not of London origin is HKL 836. This is one of three AEC Regals with Beadle bodywork that were converted by Maidstone & District to run circular tours at Hastings. Now repainted into later Hastings & District colours, it lays over at North Weald after working a trip to High Beech in Epping Forest.

The belated Steam Gala held on 11–12 September was an all Great Western affair featuring resident No. 4953 *Pitchford Hall*, visiting No. 5619 and newly visiting 57XX Pannier tank No. 5786 in London Transport livery as L92. This was one of thirteen of the class purchased by London Transport from 1956 for maintenance trains, the last of which remained in service until 1971. This is owned by the Worcester Locomotive Society and normally based on the South Devon Railway. Here she prepares to run round on arrival at Ongar. (Richard Puttock)

A demonstration freight train ran to Ongar in the morning hauled by No. 5619 and returned in the afternoon with L92. Here L92 collects the stock from the siding for the return journey on 11 September.

Right: A visitor for the Diesel Gala of 25–26 September and staying on for next month's London Transport Gala was Class 20 No. 20227 in London Transport livery owned by the Class 20 Locomotive Society. This now carries the name *Sherlock Holmes* and number 8, once carried on a Metropolitan Railway electric locomotive. Note the 221B shed plate.

Below: Visiting from the Severn Valley Railway for the Diesel Gala was Class 14 D9551, while *Pitchford Hall* had gone the other way to attend the SVR's Steam Gala. Seen laying over between duties at Ongar, the crew show how the number blinds are changed.

The climax of the gala season was the London Transport Gala held over three days, Friday–Sunday 8–10 October. This featured three locomotives in London Transport livery, probably a first for any heritage railway, along with Class 31 No. 31458. The best of the weather was on the Sunday, and here at North Weald we see No. 20227 waiting to depart for Ongar while L92 has coupled on to the rear of a train for Epping Forest headed by the Class 31 to haul it back. Note the replica London Transport roundels mounted at the stations for the occasion.

The other LT-liveried locomotive was No. 5521, alias L150, the GWR 2-6-2T making a return visit to the railway. Demonstration freight runs were made through North Weald and here the Prairie tank enters the station from the south on the Sunday afternoon.

The demonstration freight train passes through the platform with the signal at green.

Since *c.* 2019 several heritage railways have successfully adopted the idea of illuminated lights trains during the Christmas season. The EOR first tried this in 2020 but the lockdown quickly curtailed the service. This has been revised and refined for 2021. The 'Light Fantastic Train' features coloured lights on the carriages, illuminated lineside displays, on board music and narration. Evening services began from 19 November, and these are in addition to the seasonal 'Santa Specials'. L150 is seen suitably adorned en route. (Katie Pickersgill)

The Bus Services

The Epping Ongar Railway is unique in running its own bus services. As trains are not able to work into Epping station where both platforms are used by LUL, on operating days bus route 339 provides a link from Epping station to the railway at North Weald, with some journeys continuing to Ongar and (since 2014) Shenfield. The service is registered as a route so that local passengers can be carried as well. Former London Transport vehicles from the associated London Bus Company fleet are used. The route number 339 is that of the original London Transport Country Area route which ran from Warley, south of Brentwood to Harlow via Ongar and Epping.

Former Country Area RT1700 waits outside Epping station. This particular bus spent several years of its working life based at Harlow, so would have run on this route. 24 June 2013.

RTL1076 is seen turning into Epping station approach on 1 July 2013. Normally, three buses are required to maintain the 339 schedule.

In the summer holiday period a scenic route 381 via the country lanes from North Weald to Epping is offered on certain days, recreating part of another former Country Area route. On 24 June 2013 RF401 waits at North Weald, while former Green Line RT3228 prepares to set off for Ongar and another RT for Epping.

Former London Transport Green Line AEC Routemaster RCL2260 pauses at Ongar in 2018 with an afternoon service to Shenfield station. These buses originally ran on Green Line routes 721 from London to Brentwood and 722 from London to Corbets Tey, Upminster. Note the signpost pointing to the station.

Features Along the Line

Left: On display at North Weald station is this print from the painting *In the Bleak Mid-winter* by renowned transport artist Malcolm Root FGRA. This depicts the steam push-pull service at Epping as it would have been in the early 1950s and the original painting was unveiled at the railway during the 2018 Steam Gala.

Below: A close-up view of the Malcom Root print.

The replacement footbridge at North Weald is here used to artistic effect in 2017 to frame a view of the platforms. (Richard Puttock)

North Weald is the location for the loco running shed and maintenance facilities, on the site of the former goods yard. Here visiting 64XX 0-6-0PT No. 6430 stands on the pit road by the running shed on 23 April 2017. It was not in steam as this was the weekend of the Diesel Gala.

Blake Hall station building is now a private house and trains do not stop there. Part of the platform has been restored – contrast the view from 1987 (see p. 13).

Just before Ongar signal box the last remaining Finnish locomotive can be found – the Pacific. Now looking very derelict and 'named' *Dracula Castle* for a Halloween event when photographed in 2018, it was originally hoped that this would be cosmetically restored but other events have taken higher priority (see also p. 24).

The Grade II listed station building at Ongar has been restored to Great Eastern Railway colours of brown and stone as when built – believed to be the only former GER station in GER colours.

The Epping Ongar Railway won three awards in 2012 for its restoration work, and the efforts made towards this by the volunteers. The award plaques are displayed above the fireplace at Ongar station.

The fireplace at Ongar is a welcome sight when lit on a cold day. The coat of arms of the Great Eastern Railway features that of the City of London in the centre, surrounded by those of various towns, cities and counties served by the GER. This was not the original fitment at this station, which would have been of a plainer design, but has been brought in. Similar coats of arms can be found on the ironwork surrounding Liverpool Street station in London. (Andrew Cook)

A rare feature at Ongar is the foot warmer hut. This was constructed in 1896, a later addition to the station. As carriages were unheated at this time, first class passengers (only) were offered a foot warmer – a metal container filled with hot water and placed in a canvas bag, which was placed on the carriage floor for passengers to put their feet on. The foot warmers and bags were stored and heated in this hut, which had its own boiler. These foot warmers became obsolete once steam heating was fitted to carriages around the 1920s.

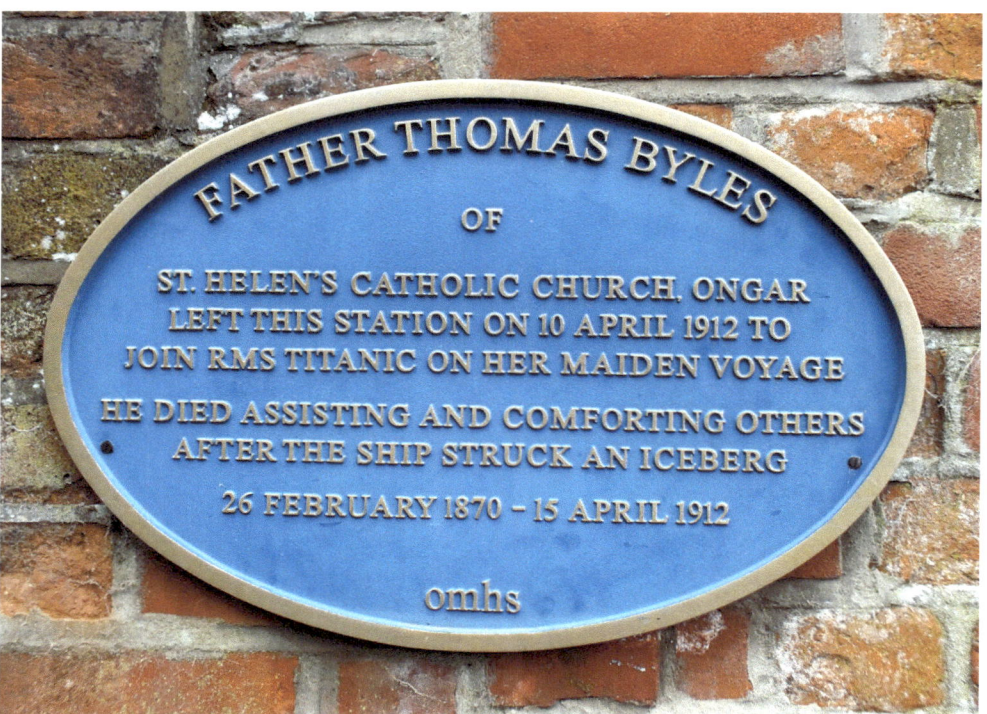

Above: This plaque at Ongar erected by the Ongar Millennium Historical Society commemorates Father Thomas Byles of St Helen's Catholic Church, Ongar. As stated, he departed from Ongar to travel to Southampton and then on the RMS *Titanic* to America where he was to officiate at his brother's wedding. When the ship hit an iceberg and sank he was offered a place in a lifeboat, but considered it his duty to comfort the dying and so went down with the ship.

Left: This cart weighbridge was installed in Ongar Goods Yard in 1889 at a cost of £155. It was discovered when the McCarthy & Stone retirement homes on the site of the coal yard were being built, and moved to its present site adjacent to the platform. Carts would be weighed laden and again when empty and the difference in weights would be charged to the merchant.

Inside the restored replacement signal box at Ongar, which was formerly at Spellbrook (see p. 26). The lever frame, however, is the original. it had been saved and stored in a barn when the previous box was demolished. (Richard Puttock)

This little Ruston 0-4-0 diesel shunter is not part of the operational fleet but has been plinthed as a 'gate guardian' at Ongar, readily visible from the high street to promote the railway.

While the majority of the goods yard land at Ongar has become housing, this pair of coal office wooden huts remain at the former entrance to the coal yard. Originally Grade II listed along with the station building in 1984, these were de-listed in 2021 and their future remains uncertain.

The Penny Salon

A new feature began in 2017 when the author, along with colleague and neighbour Geoff Silcock, converted the former ladies waiting room at Ongar, then just being used as a storeroom, into a micro-gallery that we named the Penny Salon. A regular programme of photo and other exhibitions has been presented since then featuring both our own work and guest participants.

The Penny Salon. Visitors admire part of an exhibition during 2019.

Until the final end of lockdown restrictions in July 2021, the Penny Salon could not be used, so a 'Penny Salon on tour' operated out of a chalet at North Weald with folios and framed photographs on display. Alright in sunny conditions as here, but when it rained everything had to put away quickly! Mask wearing was still the norm at this stage.

The Railway at Night

The railway takes on a whole new aspect as dusk and night approaches. On 1 January 2019 the last train has departed from Ongar, but the station and signal box are still lit up until the train clears the section and staff can start to lock up.

At certain times photographic night shoots have taken place on the railway, employing stage lighting. A night shoot in 2015 featured visiting Pannier tank No. 6430 and the autocoach seen posed in North Weald station. (Martin Creese)

The photo charter of 30 December 2019 with *Pitchford Hall* included a night shoot. This black and white scene at North Weald oozes early 1950s atmosphere. (Martin Creese)

The Future

A long-term aim would be to gain access to Epping station and connect directly with the Underground. However, at present both platforms are used by the Central Line on a daily basis. Until the Covid lockdowns of 2020–21 the car park was running at full capacity on weekdays. The Underground are under pressure to be fully accessible and access to platform 1 normally requires crossing the footbridge, So there was a possibility of a multistorey car park and a new entrance to the station further down with lifts to both platforms, allowing the EOR to take over the 1865 station building. But with passenger levels lower now due to increased homeworking, the chances of any of this happening have diminished.

> The railway has seen an increase in passenger numbers every year since 2012. However, the establishment of a direct link with London Underground at Epping would be expected to deliver far more passengers and therefore business for the local tourist economy. We would become the only heritage railway directly accessible from the Tube network and that prospect is very exciting.
> Dean Walton, EOR Business Development Manager, 2015

Epping station is the current terminus of the Central Line. The station building is of the same 1865 age and similar design pattern to stations on the Epping Ongar Railway.

In August 2016 the railway took delivery of five cast-iron roof trusses from Whitechapel station, which was being rebuilt as part of the Crossrail development. Dating from 1876, the trusses are intended to be used in a new visitor centre/café to be constructed in the remaining goods yard area at Ongar.

A classic Southern Railway poster of the past, as recreated and reinterpreted on the Epping Ongar Railway in 2021.